Contents

PATTERNS

Introduction

Welcome to the farm! My daughter, Kim, and I are so excited to have you crochet these barnyard friends with us. We worked hard to design these in such a way that even adventurous beginners can make this barnyard collection. Each design, from Bob the Dog to Quackers the Duck to Mela the Highland Cow, is made with either bulky or super bulky yarn, so they are extra squishy!

Keep in mind that gauge is important when crocheting, but with these fun-loving amigurumi animals, there is a lot of forgiveness. When working on these projects, my daughter and I had very different tensions (gauges). My gauge was tight and her gauge was loose—but all of our animals turned out adorable and hug-worthy! As long as your stitches are tight enough to not show the stuffing, you are good to go! (However, if you want them to be the exact size shown, you will need to match the gauge.)

We hope you enjoy these designs!

Best stitches,
Kristi and Kim Simpson

P.S. Everyone say "hello" to my daughter, Kim. She jumped on board and took the lead on this book! She makes my crochet-momma heart proud!

FARM FRIENDS CROCHET

Supersize Amigurumi to Cuddle and Play

KRISTI SIMPSON AND KIMBERLY SIMPSON

STACKPOLE
BOOKS
Essex, Connecticut

STACKPOLE BOOKS
The Globe Pequot Publishing Group, Inc.
64 South Main Street
Essex, CT 06426
www.globepequot.com

Copyright © 2025 by Kristi Simpson and Kimberly Simpson
Photography by Kristi Simpson

All rights reserved. No part of this book may be reproduced in any form or by any electronic or mechanical means, including information storage and retrieval systems, without written permission from the publisher, except by a reviewer who may quote passages in a review.

The contents of this book are for personal use only. Patterns herein may be reproduced in limited quantities for such use. Any large-scale commercial reproduction is prohibited without the written consent of the publisher.

We have made every effort to ensure the accuracy and completeness of these instructions. We cannot, however, be responsible for human error, typographical mistakes, or variations in individual work.

British Library Cataloguing in Publication Information available

Library of Congress Cataloging-in-Publication Data available

ISBN 9780811777155 (paperback : alk. paper) | ISBN 9780811777162 (epub)

∞™ The paper used in this publication meets the minimum requirements of American National Standard for Information Sciences—Permanence of Paper for Printed Library Materials, ANSI/NISO Z39.48-1992.

First Edition

Tips for Crochet Amigurumi Animals

When you crochet animals, consider the following tips:

- If you have gaps in your stitches, try using a smaller size hook, using a tighter tension, removing some stuffing, and/or using the invisible single crochet 2 together decrease (see Stitch Guide, page 44).
- Most of the animals in this book are designed to have one combined body and head form. The key to keeping the head from being floppy around the neckline is STUFFING! Add stuffing, then add some more! Fiberfill stuffing is available in your local craft shop or online. Alternatively, a budget-friendly option is the filling from old cushions or pillows.
- Even when adding stuffing to the arms, legs, body, or other pieces, put as much stuffing as you can into the piece all at once in one big clump, then add more to the center of the clump if needed. The key is to only add stuffing in the middle so the outside remains smooth and less lumpy. Put the stuffing in layer by layer, one on top of the other, until the piece is filled.
- Learn how to make the magic ring (sometimes called the magic circle). It allows you to pull the beginning round tightly so that there isn't a hole in your work. I have included it in the Stitch Guide on page 46 so you can see, step-by-step, how to complete this technique.
- Before adding the eyes, or any body part, stuff the body or head so you can see its shape. You can always remove the stuffing and continue your project, but it'll make the assembly easier as you complete the project.
- When joining the final round, use the invisible join (see Stitch Guide on page 45). It allows the last join to not be just a slip stitch and knot but makes the final stitch look like all the other stitches. It's easy.
- When decreasing, use the invisible single crochet 2 together (sc2tog) (see Stitch Guide on page 44). You'll love how smooth it looks compared to the traditional sc2tog.
- Count your stitches. In most of the patterns, rows and rounds vary in counts, so keep track! *Count!* It will save you time, I promise!
- Use stitch markers. Keep a stash to use to mark where the eyes will go or where you want to add the arms and legs. They can be used in many different ways beyond just marking your starting stitch.
- When sewing on your pieces, use a yarn needle or two to hold the items in place. Use them like pins to secure the pieces, or you can also use stitch markers.
- Check fiber content and care instructions especially when there is more than one yarn in a project.
- ***Important safety note:*** Never attach anything to a toddler's or baby's toy or doll that can be pulled or chewed off and swallowed. I have used safety eyes on most of the animals, but a simple crocheted round eye, or circle, can be used instead.

Notes on the Instructions

- When a number appears before the stitch name, such as 3 dc, work these stitches into the same stitch, for example "3 dc into the next st."
- When only one stitch is to be worked into each of a number of stitches, it can be written like this, for example, "1 sc in each of next 3 sts." When a number appears after a chain, for example, ch 10, this means work the number of chains indicated.
- The asterisks mark a specific set of instructions that are repeated, for example, "*2 sc in next st, 1 dc in next st, rep from * across," means repeat the stitches from the asterisk to next given instruction.
- When instructions are given with parentheses, it can mean three things: First, for example, "(2 dc, ch 1, 2 dc) in the next st" means work 2 dc, ch 1, 2 dc all into the same stitch. It can also mean a set of stitches repeated a number of times, for example, "(sc in next st, 2 sc in next st) 6 times." Last, the number(s) given at the end of a row or round in the parentheses denote(s) the number of stitches or spaces you should have on that row or round.
- Be sure to read the Special Stitch(es) and Pattern Note(s) sections, if any, before beginning a project. You'll find any new stitches and helpful hints there, and reading these notes will often clear up any questions about the project.

Abbreviations

blo	back loop only
ch(s)	chain/chains
ch-	refers to chain or space previously made
dc	double crochet
flo	front loop only
hdc	half double crochet
rep(s)	repeat(s)
rnd(s)	round(s)
RS	right side
sc	single crochet
sc2tog	single crochet 2 stitches together
sk	skip
sl st(s)	slip stitch(es)
sp(s)	space(s)
st(s)	stitch(es)
tog	together
WS	wrong side

BOB THE DOG

Bob the Dog is the farmer's best friend. He's filled with courage and bravery, and he protects the other animals. He loves roaming the farm and taking naps in the barn. Topped with his favorite bandana and hat, Bob is ready for a hard day's work!

Yarn

Cascade Lana Grande; super bulky weight #6; 100% Peruvian Highland wool; 3.5 oz. (100 g)/87.5 yd. (80 m) per skein: 6 skeins in 6029 Sienna (A)

Cascade Anthem Chunky; bulky weight #5; 100% acrylic; 7.05 oz. (200 g)/218 yd. (200 m) per skein: 1 skein each in 41 Denim (B), 07 Silver (C), 05 Black (D)

Hook and Other Materials

US size J-10 (6 mm) crochet hook
Yarn needle
Fiberfill stuffing
Two 15 mm safety eyes
Stitch markers

Finished Measurements

About 16½ in. (41.9 cm) high (not counting hat)

Gauge

11 sc and 11 rows/rounds = 4 in. (10 cm)

Pattern Note

- Dog is made in 9 pieces: Body and Head, 2 Legs, 2 Arms, Muzzle, 2 Ears, and Tail.

INSTRUCTIONS

Body

Rnd 1 (RS): With A, ch 2, 8 sc in 2nd ch from hook; do not join. (8 sc) Place marker to indicate beginning of rnd.

Note: Loop a short piece of yarn around any stitch to mark Rnd 1 as right side. Move stitch marker up with each rnd.

Rnd 2: 2 sc in each st around. (16 sc)

Rnd 3: (Sc in next st, 2 sc in next st) around. (24 sc)

Rnd 4: (Sc in next 2 sts, 2 sc in next st) around. (32 sc)
Rnd 5: (Sc in next 3 sts, 2 sc in next st) around. (40 sc)
Rnd 6: (Sc in next 4 sts, 2 sc in next st) around. (48 sc)
Rnd 7: (Sc in next 5 sts, 2 sc in next st) around. (56 sc)
Rnd 8: (Sc in next 6 sts, 2 sc in next st) around. (64 sc)
Rnds 9–30: Sc in each st around.
Rnd 31: (Sc in next 6 sts, sc2tog) around. (56 sc)
Rnd 32: Sc in each st around.
Rnd 33: (Sc in next 5 sts, sc2tog) around. (48 sc)
Rnd 34: Sc in each st around.
Rnd 35: (Sc in next 4 sts, sc2tog) around. (40 sc)
Rnd 36: (Sc in next 3 sts, sc2tog) around. (32 sc)
Rnd 37: (Sc in next 2 sts, sc2tog) around. (24 sc)
Stuff Body.

Head

Rnd 38: 2 sc in each st around. (48 sc)
Rnd 39: (Sc in next 5 sts, 2 sc in next st) around. (56 sc)
Rnd 40: (Sc in next 6 sts, 2 sc in next st) around. (64 sc)
Rnds 41–53: Sc in each sc around.
Rnd 54: (Sc in next 6 sts, sc2tog) around. (56 sc)
Add safety eyes between Rnds 51 and 55 about 5 sts apart.
Rnd 55: Sc in each st around.
Rnd 56: (Sc in next 5 sts, sc2tog) around. (48 sc)
Rnd 57: (Sc in next 4 sts, sc2tog) around. (40 sc)
Rnd 58: (Sc in next 3 sts, sc2tog) around. (32 sc)
Rnd 59: (Sc in next 2 sts, sc2tog) around. (24 sc)
Stuff Head.
Rnd 60: (Sc in next st, sc2tog) around. (16 sc)
Rnd 61: (Sc2tog) 8 times. Fasten off, leaving a long tail.
Use yarn needle and long tail to sew Rnd 61 closed.

Leg (make 2)

Rnd 1 (RS): With A, ch 2, 5 sc in second ch from hook, do not join. (5 sc) Place marker to indicate beginning of rnd.
Note: Loop a short piece of yarn around any stitch to mark Rnd 1 as right side. Move stitch marker up with each rnd.
Rnd 2: 2 sc in each st around. (10 sc)
Rnd 3: (Sc in next st, 2 sc in next st) around. (15 sc)
Rnd 4: (Sc in next 2 sts, 2 sc in next st) around. (20 sc)
Rnd 5: (Sc in next 3 sts, 2 sc in next st) around. (25 sc)
Rnd 6: Sc in each st around.
Rnd 7: Sc2tog, sc in each st around. (24 sc)
Rnd 8: (Sc in next 2 sts, sc2tog) around. (18 sc)
Rnds 9–14: Sc in each st around.
Rnd 15: (Sc in next 7 sts, sc2tog) around. (16 sc)
Rnds 16–23: Sc in each st around. Fasten off, leaving a long tail for sewing.
Stuff firmly at paw section, lightly stuff Leg, and leave remaining 2½ in. (6.4 cm) unstuffed.

Arm (make 2)

Rnd 1: With A, ch 2, 5 sc in second ch from hook, do not join. (5 sc) Place marker to indicate beginning of rnd.
Note: Loop a short piece of yarn around any stitch to mark Rnd 1 as right side. Move stitch marker up with each rnd.
Rnd 2: 2 sc in each st around. (10 sc)
Rnd 3: (Sc in next st, 2 sc in next st) around. (15 sc)
Rnd 4: (Sc in next 2 sts, 2 sc in next st) around. (20 sc)
Rnd 5: Sc in each st around.
Rnd 6: (Sc in next 2 sts, sc2tog) around. (15 sc)
Rnds 7–22: Sc in each st around. Fasten off, leaving a long tail for sewing.
Stuff firmly at paw section, lightly stuff Arm, and leave remaining 2½ in. (6.4 cm) unstuffed.

Muzzle

Rnd 1 (RS): With A, ch 6, 2 sc in second ch from hook, sc in next 3 chs, 4 sc in last ch, working on opposite side of chain in free loops, sc in next 3 chs, 2 sc in last ch, join with slip st to first sc. (14 sc)
Note: Loop a short piece of yarn around any stitch to mark Rnd 1 as right side. Move stitch marker up with each rnd.
Rnd 2: Ch 1, sc in same st as joining, 2 sc in next st, sc in next 3 sts, 2 sc in next st, sc in next 2 sts, 2 sc in next st, sc in next 3 sts, 2 sc in next st, sc in last st, join with slip st to first sc. (18 sc)
Rnd 3: Ch 1, sc in same st as joining and in next st, 2 sc in next st, sc in next 4 sts, 2 sc in next st, sc in next 3 sts, 2 sc in next st, sc in next 4 sts, 2 sc in next st, sc in last st, join with slip st to first sc. (22 sc)
Rnds 4–7: Ch 1, sc in same st as joining and in each st around, join with slip st to first sc. Fasten off, leaving a long tail for sewing.
Stuff Muzzle.

Ear (make 2)

Row 1 (RS): With A, ch 4, 2 sc in second ch from hook, sc in next ch, 2 sc in last ch. (5 sc)

Note: Loop a short piece of yarn around any stitch to mark Row 1 as right side.

Row 2: Ch 1, turn; sc in each st across.

Row 3: Ch 1, turn; 2 sc in first st, sc in next 3 sts, 2 sc in last st. (7 sc)

Rows 4 and 5: Ch 1, turn; sc in each st across.

Row 6: Ch 1, turn; 2 sc in first st, sc in next 5 sts, 2 sc in last st. (9 sc)

Rows 7–10: Ch 1, turn; sc in each st across.

Row 11: Ch 1, turn; 2 sc in first st, sc in next 7 sts, 2 sc in last st. (11 sc)

Rows 12–16: Ch 1, turn; sc in each st across.

Trim: Ch 1, turn; sc in each st across, work 16 sc across ends of rows, work 5 sc across foundation chains of Row 1, work 16 sc across ends of rows; join with slip st to first sc. Fasten off.

Tail

Row 1 (RS): With A, ch 8, sc in second ch from hook and in each ch across. (7 sc)

Note: Loop a short piece of yarn around any stitch to mark Row 1 as right side.

Rows 2–4: Ch 1, turn; sc in each st across. Fasten off, leaving a long tail for sewing.

Use yarn needle and long tail to sew Row 1 and 4 together.

Cut eight 4-in. (10-cm) strands of yarn. Join as fringe on one end of Tail by folding yarn in half and pulling loop through the ends of a stitch. Pull ends through loop and tighten. Trim evenly.

Bandana

With B, make a magic ring.

Row 1 (RS): Work (ch 3, 2 dc, ch 2, 3 dc) in ring.

Note: Loop a short piece of yarn around any stitch to mark Row 1 as right side.

Row 2: Ch 3 (counts as dc throughout), turn; 2 dc in same st, ch 1, (3 dc, ch 2, 3 dc) in ch-2 sp, ch 1, 3 dc in top of turning ch.

Row 3: Ch 3, turn; 2 dc in same st, ch 1, 3 dc in next ch-1 sp, ch 1, (3 dc, ch 2, 3 dc) in ch-2 sp, ch 1, 3 dc in next ch-1 sp, ch 1, 3 dc in top of turning ch.

Row 4: Ch 3, 2 dc in same st, *ch 1, 3 dc in next ch-1 sp*, rep from * to * to next ch-2 sp, ch 1, (3 dc, ch 2, 3 dc) in ch-2 sp, repeat from * to * across, 3 dc in top of turning ch.

Rows 5–8: Rep Row 4. Fasten off.

Ties

Join B at the end of each side of Row 8, ch 21. Fasten off.

Hat

Rnd 1 (RS): With B, ch 2, 6 sc in second ch from hook; do not join. (6 sc) Place marker to indicate beginning of rnd.

Note: Loop a short piece of yarn around any stitch to mark Rnd 1 as right side. Move stitch marker up with each rnd.

Rnd 2: 2 sc in each st around. (12 sc)

Rnd 3: (Sc in next st, 2 sc in next st) around. (18 sc)

Rnd 4: (Sc in next 2 sts, 2 sc in next st) around. (24 sc)

Rnd 5: (Sc in next 3 sts, 2 sc in next st) around. (30 sc)

Rnd 6: (Sc in next 4 sts, 2 sc in next st) around. (36 sc)

Rnds 7–10: Sc in each st around.

Rnd 11: Sc in each st around; join with slip st to first st. Fasten off, leaving a long tail for sewing.

Bill

Row 1 (RS): Join C with slip st in any st in the flo, ch 1, sc in same st as joining and in next 11 sts. (12 sc)

Note: Loop a short piece of yarn around any stitch to mark Row 1 as right side.

Rows 2 and 3: Ch 1, turn; sc in each st across.

Row 4: Ch 1, beginning with first st, sc3tog, sc in next 6 sts, sc3tog. (8 sc)

Row 5: Ch 1, beginning with first st, sc2tog, sc 4, sc2tog. (6 sc) Fasten off.

Trim: Join C in same st as beginning Row 1, ch 1, work 5 sc in ends of rows on edge of Bill, sc 6 across Row 5, work 5 sc in ends of rows on edge of Bill, slip st in same st as last st of Row 1. Fasten off, leaving a long tail for sewing.

Assembly

Use photos as a guide.

Sew Muzzle on Head, stuffing before closing.

With D, stitch nose on Muzzle.

Sew Ears on Head.

Sew Arms and Legs on Body.

Tack Legs to Body to hold in place.

Sew Tail on lower middle back.

Sew Hat on Head between Ears, stuffing before closing.

Tie on Bandana.

TESSA THE PIG

Tessa the Pig is always dressed and ready for lunch. Her meals are served on time or she gets pushy. Her skirt is always nice and neat and her bow tidy. She loves snuggles and a good mud bath!

Yarn

Cascade Cherub Chunky; bulky weight #5; 55% nylon/45% acrylic; 3.5 oz. (100 g)/136.7 yd. (125 m) per skein: 2 skeins in 04 Baby Pink (A); 1 skein each in 17 Grey (B), 45 Raspberry (C), 01 White (D), 40 Black (E) (scrap for eyelashes)

Hook and Other Materials

US size H (5 mm) crochet hook
Yarn needle
Fiberfill stuffing
Two 15 mm safety eyes
Stitch markers

Finished Measurements

About 14½ in. (36.8 cm) high (not counting Ears)

Gauge

18 sc and 18 rows/rounds = 4 in. (10 cm)

Pattern Note

- All yarns of the same weight designation are not created equal. This yarn is on the thinner side of bulky weight #5. You can use any yarn, though, as long as your stitches are tight. This gauge is tighter than the other animals and is closer to a medium weight gauge.

INSTRUCTIONS

Body

Rnd 1 (RS): With A, ch 2, 8 sc in 2nd ch from hook, do not join. (8 sc) Place marker to indicate beginning of rnd.

Note: Loop a short piece of yarn around any stitch to mark Rnd 1 as right side. Move stitch marker up with each rnd.

Rnd 2: 2 sc in each st around. (16 sc)
Rnd 3: (Sc in next st, 2 sc in next st) around. (24 sc)
Rnd 4: (Sc in next 2 sts, 2 sc in next st) around. (32 sc)
Rnd 5: (Sc in next 3 sts, 2 sc in next st) around. (40 sc)
Rnd 6: (Sc in next 4 sts, 2 sc in next st) around. (48 sc)
Rnd 7: (Sc in next 5 sts, 2 sc in next st) around. (56 sc)
Rnd 8: (Sc in next 6 sts, 2 sc in next st) around. (64 sc)
Rnd 9: (Sc in next 7 sts, 2 sc in next st) around. (72 sc)
Rnd 10: Sc in each st around.
Rnd 11: (Sc in next 8 sts, 2 sc in next st) around. (80 sc)
Rnds 12–23: Sc in each st around.
Rnd 24: Sc in each st around, join with slip st to first sc. Fasten off.
Rnd 25: Join B with slip st, ch 1, sc in same st as joining and in each st around, join with slip st to first sc. Fasten off.
Rnd 26: Join C with slip st in the back loop, ch 1, working in blo, sc in same st as joining and in each st around, join with slip st to first sc.
Rnd 27: Ch 1, working in both loops, sc in same st as joining and in each st around, do not join.
Rnd 28: Sc in each st around.
Rnd 29: (Sc in next 8 sts, sc2tog) around. (72 sc)
Rnds 30–32: Sc in each st around.
Rnd 33: (Sc in next 7 sts, sc2tog) around. (64 sc)
Rnds 34–36: Sc in each st around.
Rnd 37: (Sc in next 6 sts, sc2tog) around. (56 sc)
Rnds 38 and 39: Sc in each st around.
Rnd 40: (Sc in next 5 sts, sc2tog) around. (48 sc)
Rnds 41 and 42: Sc in each st around.
Rnd 43: (Sc in next 4 sts, sc2tog) around. (40 sc)
Rnds 44 and 45: Sc in each st around.
Rnd 46: (Sc in next 4 sts, sc2tog) around. (32 sc)
Rnd 47: (Sc in next 3 sts, sc2tog) around. (24 sc) Fasten off.
Rnd 48: Join A with slip st, ch 1, sc in same st as joining and in each st around, join with slip st to first sc.

Head

Rnd 49: Ch 1, 2 sc in same st as joining and in each st around, do not join. (48 sc)
Rnd 50: (Sc in next 5 sts, 2 sc in next st) around. (56 sc)
Rnd 51: (Sc in next 6 sts, 2 sc in next st) around. (64 sc)
Rnd 52: (Sc in next 7 sts, 2 sc in next st) around. (72 sc)
Rnds 53–70: Sc in each st around.
Attach safety eyes between Rnds 63 and 64 about 6 sts apart.
Rnd 71: (Sc in next 7 sts, sc2tog) around. (64 sc)
Rnd 72: Sc in each st around.
Rnd 73: (Sc in next 6 sts, sc2tog) around. (56 sc)
Rnd 74: Sc in each st around.
Rnd 75: (Sc in next 5 sts, sc2tog) around. (48 sc)
Rnd 76: (Sc in next 4 sts, sc2tog) around. (40 sc)
Rnd 77: (Sc in next 3 sts, sc2tog) around. (32 sc)
Rnd 78: (Sc in next 2 sts, sc2tog) around. (24 sc)
Rnd 79: (Sc in next st, sc2tog) around. (16 sc)
Rnd 80: (Sc2tog) 8 times. (8 sc) Fasten off, leaving a long tail for sewing.
Use yarn needle and long tail to sew Rnd 80 closed.

Nose

Rnd 1 (RS): With A, create a magic ring, work 8 sc in ring, join with slip st to first sc. (8 sc)
Note: Loop a short piece of yarn around any stitch to mark Rnd 1 as right side. Move stitch marker up with each rnd.
Rnd 2: Ch 1, 2 sc in same st as joining and in each st around, join with slip st to first sc. (16 sc)
Rnd 3: Ch 1, sc in same st as joining, 2 sc in next st, (sc in next st, 2 sc in next st) around, join with slip st to blo of first sc. (24 sc)
Rnd 4: Ch 1, working in blo, sc in same st as joining and in each st around; join with slip st to both loops of first sc.
Rnd 5: Ch 1, sc in same st as joining and in each st around; join with slip st to first sc. Fasten off, leaving a long tail for sewing.

Ear (make 2)

Row 1 (WS): With A, ch 3, sc in second ch from hook and in next ch. (2 sc)
Row 2 (RS): Ch 1, turn; 2 sc in each st across. (4 sc)
Note: Loop a short piece of yarn around any stitch to mark Row 2 as right side.
Row 3: Ch 1, turn; sc in each st across.
Row 4: Ch 1, turn; 2 sc in first st, sc in next 2 sts, 2 sc in last st. (6 sc)
Row 5: Ch 1, turn; sc in each st across.
Row 6: Ch 1, turn; 2 sc in first st, sc in next 4 sts, 2 sc in last st. (8 sc)
Rows 7–11: Ch 1, turn; sc in each st across.

Trim: Ch 1, work 11 sc on ends of rows, work 2 sc across foundation ch on Rnd 1, work 11 sc on ends of rows; join with slip st to first st of Row 11. Fasten off, leaving a long tail for sewing.

Leg (make 2)

Rnd 1 (RS): With A, ch 2, 6 sc in second ch from hook; do not join. (6 sc) Place marker to indicate beginning of rnd.

Note: Loop a short piece of yarn around any stitch to mark Rnd 1 as right side. Move stitch marker up with each rnd.

Rnd 2: 2 sc in each st around. (12 sc)

Rnd 3: (Sc in next st, 2 sc in next st) around. (18 sc)

Rnd 4: (Sc in next 2 sts, 2 sc in next st) around. (24 sc)

Rnds 5–10: Sc in each st around.

Rnd 11: (Sc in next 4 sts, sc2tog) around. (20 sc)

Rnds 12–25: Sc in each st around. Fasten off, leaving a long tail for sewing.

Stuff firmly at paw section, lightly stuff Leg, and leave remaining 2½ in. (6.4 cm) unstuffed.

Arm (make 2)

Rnd 1 (RS): With A, ch 2, 5 sc in second ch from hook; do not join. (5 sc) Place marker to indicate beginning of rnd.

Note: Loop a short piece of yarn around any stitch to mark Rnd 1 as right side. Move stitch marker up with each rnd.

Rnd 2: 2 sc in each st around. (10 sc)

Rnd 3: (Sc in next st, 2 sc in next st) around. (15 sc)

Rnd 4: (Sc in next 2 sts, 2 sc in next st) around. (20 sc)

Rnd 5: Sc in each st around.

Rnd 6: (Sc in next 3 sts, sc2tog) around. (16 sc)

Rnds 7–14: Sc in each st around. Fasten off.

Rnd 15: Join C with slip st, ch 1, sc in same st as joining, sc in each st around, join with slip st to first sc.

Rnd 16: Ch 1, sc in same st as joining, sc in each st around, do not join.

Rnds 17–20: Sc in each st around. Fasten off, leaving a long tail for sewing.

Stuff firmly at paw section, lightly stuff Arm, and leave remaining 2½ in. (6.4 cm) unstuffed.

Tail

Row 1 (RS): With A, ch 10, 3 sc in second ch from hook and in each ch across. (27 sc)

Shirt Flower

Rnd 1 (RS): With B, ch 2, 7 sc in second ch from hook; join with slip st to first sc. (7 sc) Fasten off.

Note: Loop a short piece of yarn around any stitch to mark Rnd 1 as right side.

Rnd 2: Join D with slip st in any st, (ch 1, dc, ch 1, sl st) in same st, (sl st, ch 1, dc, ch 1, sl st) in each st around, join with slip st to first st. (7 petals) Fasten off, leaving a long tail for sewing.

Ear Flower

Rnd 1 (RS): With C, ch 2, 6 sc in second ch from hook, join with slip st to first sc. (6 sc)

Note: Loop a short piece of yarn around any stitch to mark Rnd 1 as right side.

Rnd 2: (Ch 1, dc, ch 1, sl st) in same st as joining, (sl st, ch 1, dc, ch 1, sl st) in each st around; join with slip st to first st. (6 petals) Fasten off, leaving a long tail for sewing.

Skirt

Rnd 1 (RS): With the Head facing down, join B in back exposed loop from Rnd 26 of Body, ch 3 (counts as dc throughout), dc in same st as joining, *sk 1 st, 2 dc in next st, repeat from * around, sk 1 st, join with slip st to the space between the beginning ch-3 and first dc. (80 dc)

Note: Loop a short piece of yarn around any stitch to mark Rnd 1 as right side.

Rnd 2: Ch 4 (first dc and ch 1), dc in same sp, sk next 2 dc, *(dc, ch 1, dc) in space between last skipped dc and next dc, repeat from * around, join with slip st in first ch-1 sp.

Rnds 3–6: Ch 4, dc in same sp, (dc, ch 1, dc) in each ch-1 sp around, join with slip st to first ch-1 sp. [80 (dc, ch 1, dc) groups]

Rnd 7: (Ch 1, dc, ch 1, slip st) in same sp, (sl st, ch 1, dc, ch 1, sl st) in each ch-1 sp around, join with slip st to first st. (80 petals) Fasten off.

Assembly

Use photos as a guide.

Sew Nose on Head, stuffing before closing.

With E and yarn needle, make eyelashes on the edge of safety eyes.

Sew Ears on Head.

Sew Flower on Ear.

Sew Arms and Legs on Body.

Tack Legs to Body to hold in place.

Sew Shirt Flower on Body.

Sew Tail on lower back of Body at bottom of Skirt (so the Tail will be seen).

MOLLY THE COW

Moooove over for this adorable cow! She's ready for her hay and a dip in the pond. She's super squishy and enjoys a good head scratch. She loves to roam the pasture and relax in the barn. Bread is her favorite treat, so don't forget it!

Yarn

Cascade Anthem Chunky; bulky weight #5; 100% acrylic; 7.05 oz. (200 g)/218 yd. (200 m) per skein: 2 skeins in 08 White (A); 1 skein each in 05 Black (B), 07 Silver (D), 21 Gold (F)

Cascade Cherub Chunky; bulky weight #5; 55% nylon/45% acrylic; 3.5 oz. (100 g)/136.7 yd. (125 m) per skein: 1 skein each in 04 Baby Pink (C), 45 Raspberry (E)

Hook and Other Materials

US size 10.5 (6.5 mm) crochet hook
Yarn needle
Fiberfill stuffing
Two 15 mm safety eyes
Stitch markers

Finished Measurements

About 17 in. (43.2 cm) high (not counting hat)

Gauge

11 sc and 11 rows/rounds = 4 in. (10 cm)

INSTRUCTIONS

Body

Rnd 1 (RS): With A, ch 2, 8 sc in 2nd ch from hook, do not join. (8 sc) Place marker to indicate beginning of rnd.

Note: Loop a short piece of yarn around any stitch to mark Rnd 1 as right side. Move stitch marker up with each rnd.

Rnd 2: 2 sc in each st around. (16 sc)

Rnd 3: (Sc in next st, 2 sc in next st) around. (24 sc)

Rnd 4: (Sc in next 2 sts, 2 sc in next st) around. (32 sc)

Rnd 5: (Sc in next 3 sts, 2 sc in next st) around. (40 sc)
Rnd 6: (Sc in next 4 sts, 2 sc in next st) around. (48 sc)
Rnd 7: (Sc in next 5 sts, 2 sc in next st) around. (56 sc)
Rnd 8: (Sc in next 6 sts, 2 sc in next st) around. (64 sc)
Rnds 9–30: Sc in each st around.
Rnd 31: (Sc in next 6 sts, sc2tog) around. (56 sc)
Rnd 32: Sc in each st around.
Rnd 33: (Sc in next 5 sts, sc2tog) around. (48 sc)
Rnd 34: Sc in each st around.
Rnd 35: (Sc in next 4 sts, sc2tog) around. (40 sc)
Rnd 36: (Sc in next 3 sts, sc2tog) around. (32 sc)
Rnd 37: (Sc in next 2 sts, sc2tog) around. (24 sc)
Stuff Body.

Head

Rnd 38: 2 sc in each st around. (48 sc)
Rnd 39: (Sc in next 5 sts, 2 sc in next st) around. (56 sc)
Rnd 40: (Sc in next 6 sts, 2 sc in next st) around. (64 sc)
Rnds 41–53: Sc in each sc around.
Rnd 54: (Sc in next 6 sts, sc2tog) around. (56 sc)

Add safety eyes between Rnds 52 and 53 about 5 sts apart.
Rnd 55: Sc in each st around.
Rnd 56: (Sc in next 5 sts, sc2tog) around. (48 sc)
Rnd 57: (Sc in next 4 sts, sc2tog) around. (40 sc)
Rnd 58: (Sc in next 3 sts, sc2tog) around. (32 sc)
Rnd 59: (Sc in next 2 sts, sc2tog) around. (24 sc)
Stuff Head.
Rnd 60: (Sc in next st, sc2tog) around. (16 sc)
Rnd 61: (Sc2tog) 8 times. Fasten off, leaving a long tail.
Use yarn needle and long tail to sew Rnd 61 closed.

Leg (make 2)

Rnd 1 (RS): With B, ch 2, 5 sc in second ch from hook, do not join. (5 sc) Place marker to indicate beginning of rnd.
Note: Loop a short piece of yarn around any stitch to mark Rnd 1 as right side. Move stitch marker up with each rnd.
Rnd 2: 2 sc in each st around. (10 sc)
Rnd 3: (Sc in next st, 2 sc in next st) around. (15 sc)
Rnd 4: (Sc in next 2 sts, 2 sc in next st) around. (20 sc)
Rnd 5: (Sc in next 3 sts, 2 sc in next st) around. (25 sc)
Rnd 6: Sc in each st around. Fasten off.
Rnd 7: Join A with slip st in any st, ch 1, sc2tog, sc in each st around. (24 sc)
Rnd 8: (Sc in next 2 sts, sc2tog) around. (18 sc)
Rnds 9–14: Sc in each st around.
Rnd 15: (Sc in next 7 sts, sc2tog) around. (16 sc)
Rnds 16–23: Sc in each st around. Fasten off, leaving a long tail for sewing.
Stuff firmly at hoof section, lightly stuff Leg, and leave remaining 2½ in. (6.4 cm) unstuffed.

Arm (make 2)

Rnd 1 (RS): With B, ch 2, 5 sc in second ch from hook, do not join. (5 sc) Place marker to indicate beginning of rnd.
Note: Loop a short piece of yarn around any stitch to mark Rnd 1 as right side. Move stitch marker up with each rnd.
Rnd 2: 2 sc in each st around. (10 sc)
Rnd 3: (Sc in next st, 2 sc in next st) around. (15 sc)
Rnd 4: (Sc in next 2 sts, 2 sc in next st) around. (20 sc)
Rnd 5: Sc in each st around. Fasten off.
Rnd 6: Join A with slip st in any st, ch 1, sc in same st as joining, sc in next st, sc2tog, (sc in next 2 sts, sc2tog) around. (15 sc)

Rnds 7–22: Sc in each st around. Fasten off, leaving a long tail for sewing.

Stuff firmly at hoof section, lightly stuff Arm and leave remaining 2½ in. (6.4 cm) unstuffed.

Nose

Rnd 1 (RS): With C, ch 17, 2 sc in second ch from hook, sc in next 14 ch, 4 sc in last ch, working on opposite side of chain in free loops, sc in next 14 chs, 2 sc in last ch, join with slip st to first sc. (36 sc)

Note: Loop a short piece of yarn around any stitch to mark Rnd 1 as right side. Move stitch marker up with each rnd.

Rnd 2: Ch 1, sc in same st as joining, 2 sc in next st, sc in next 14 sc, 2 sc in next st, sc in next 2 sts, 2 sc in next st, sc in next 14 sts, 2 sc in next st, sc in last st, join with slip st to first st. (40 sc)

Rnd 3: Ch 1, sc in same st as joining and in next st, 2 sc in next st, sc in next 14 sts, 2 sc in next st, sc in next 4 sts, 2 sc in next st, sc in next 14 sts, 2 sc in next st, sc in next 2 sts, join with slip st to first st. (44 sc)

Rnds 4–6: Ch 1, sc in same st as joining and in each st around, join with slip st to first st. Fasten off, leaving a long tail for sewing.

Cap Nose with B, sew an X on each side of the nose.

Ear (make 2)

Rnd 1 (RS): With B, ch 2, work 4 sc in second ch from hook, do not join. (4 sc) Place marker to indicate beginning of rnd.

Note: Loop a short piece of yarn around any stitch to mark Rnd 1 as right side. Move stitch marker up with each rnd.

Rnd 2: 2 sc in each st around. (8 sc)

Rnd 3: Sc in each st around.

Rnd 4: (Sc in next st, 2 sc in next st) around. (12 sc)

Rnd 5: (Sc in next 2 sts, 2 sc in next st) around. (16 sc)

Rnd 6: Sc in each st around.

Rnd 7: (Sc in next 3 sts, 2 sc in next st) around. (20 sc)

Rnds 8–10: Sc in each st around.

Rnd 11: (Sc in next 3 sts, sc2tog) around. (16 sc)

Rnd 12: (Sc in next 2 sts, sc2tog) around. (12 sc) Fasten off, leaving a long tail for sewing.

Do not stuff.

Bell

Rnd 1 (RS): With D, ch 2, work 4 sc in second ch from hook, join with slip st to first sc. (4 sc)

Note: Loop a short piece of yarn around any stitch to mark Rnd 1 as right side.

Rnd 2: Ch 1, 2 sc in same st as joining and in each st around, join with slip st to first sc. (8 sc)

Rnd 3: Ch 1, sc in same st as joining and in each st around, join with slip st to first sc.

Rnd 4: Ch 1, sc in same st as joining, 2 sc in next st, (sc in next st, 2 sc in next st) around, join with slip st to first sc. (12 sc)

Rnd 5: Ch 1, sc in same st as joining and in each st around, join with slip st to first sc.

Rnd 6: Ch 1, sc in same st as joining and in next st, 2 sc in next st, (sc in next 2 sc, 2 sc in next st) around, join with slip st to first sc. (16 sc)

Rnd 7: Ch 1, sc in same st as joining and in each st around, join with slip st to first sc.

Rnd 8: Ch 1, sc in same st as joining and in next 2 sts, 2 sc in next st, (sc in next 3 sts, 2 sc in next st) around, join with slip st to first sc. (20 sc) Fasten off.

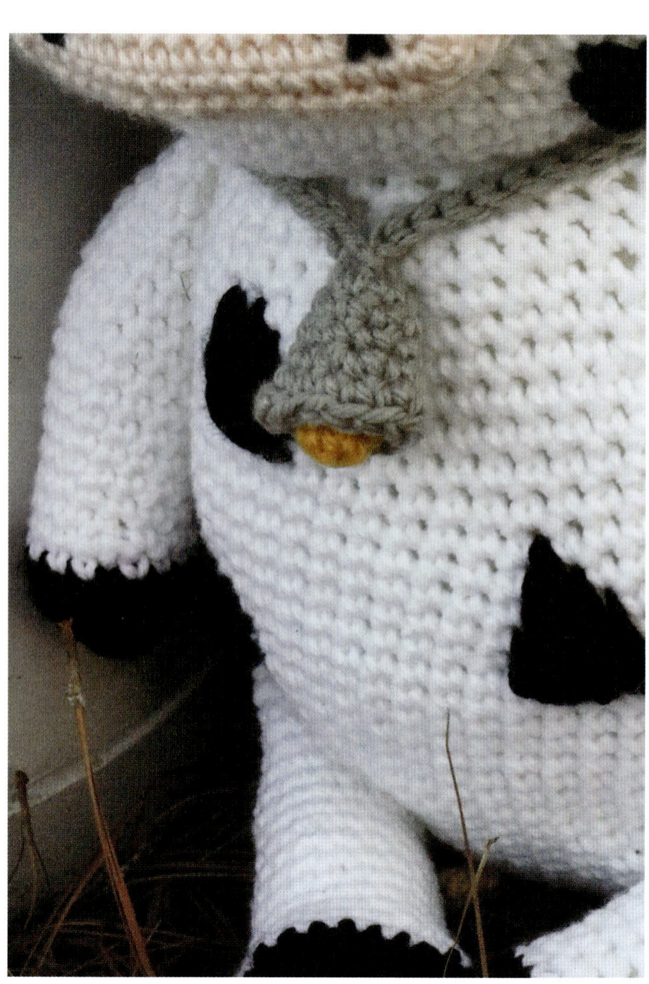

Bell Center

Rnd 1 (RS): With F, ch 2, work 5 sc in second ch from hook, do not join. (5 sc) Place marker to indicate beginning of rnd.

Note: Loop a short piece of yarn around any stitch to mark Rnd 1 as right side.

Rnd 2: 2 sc in each st around. (10 sc)

Rnds 3 and 4: Sc in each st around.

Rnd 5: (Sc2tog) 5 times. (5 sc)

Stuff Bell Center.

Fasten off.

Thread yarn needle with long length of E, insert Bell Center in Bell, and sew in place.

Bell Collar

With D, ch 57, slip st in second ch from hook and in each ch across. Fasten off, leaving a long tail.

Thread yarn needle with long tail and sew together and over top center of Bell.

Bow

Rnd 1: With E, ch 29, sc in second ch from hook and in each ch across, join with slip st to first sc. (28 sc)

Note: Loop a short piece of yarn around any stitch to mark Rnd 1 as right side.

Rnds 2 and 3: Ch 3 (counts as first dc), dc in each st around; join with slip st to beginning ch 3.

Rnd 4: Ch 1, sc in same st as joining and in each st around, join with slip st to first sc. Fasten off, leaving a long tail for sewing.

Fold Bow in half with slip st seam in middle, wrap long end tightly around center 10 times, secure. Leave a long tail for sewing.

Assembly

Use photos as a guide.

Sew Nose on Head, stuffing before closing.

With B and yarn needle, make eyelashes on the edge of safety eyes.

Sew Ears on Head.

Sew Arms and Legs on Body.

Tack Legs to Body to hold in place.

With B, embroider satin stitch "spots" on Body, Head, Arms, and Legs.

Tail

Cut 6 strands of B, each 12 in. (30.4 cm) long.

Fold in half, pull center loop through stitch in lower back of Body, pull ends through loop and tighten. Separate ends into 3 even sections and braid. Knot and trim.

Hair

Cut 15 strands of B, each 6 in. (15.2 cm) long.

Cut 6 strands of D, each 6 in. (15.2 cm) long.

Add as fringe at top of Head in the same way you made the Tail.

Wrap Hair with strand of B 5 times and knot tightly 1 in. (2.5 cm) from Head to secure and help hold Hair up in a pixie style.

Sew Bow to wrap on hair.

Trim Hair evenly.

SANDY THE CHICKEN

Sandy is the sassiest chicken you'll ever meet. Her dainty feathers are never out of place, and she's always ready to cross the road. She loves her early morning schedule and never misses cuddle time.

Yarn

Cascade Anthem Chunky; bulky weight #5; 100% acrylic; 7.05 oz. (200 g)/218 yd. (200 m) per skein: 2 skeins in 08 White (A); 1 skein each in 21 Gold (B), 03 Red (C), 07 Silver (D), 41 Denim (E), 05 Black (F) (scrap for eyelashes)

Hook and Other Materials

US size J-10 (6 mm) crochet hook
Yarn needle
Fiberfill stuffing
Two 15 mm safety eyes
Stitch markers

Finished Measurements

About 14½ in. (36.8 cm) high (not counting Comb)

Gauge

13 sc and 13 rows/rounds = 4 in. (10 cm)

INSTRUCTIONS

Body

Rnd 1 (RS): With A, ch 2, 8 sc in 2nd ch from hook, do not join. (8 sc) Place marker to indicate beginning of rnd.

Note: Loop a short piece of yarn around any stitch to mark Rnd 1 as right side. Move stitch marker up with each rnd.

Rnd 2: 2 sc in each st around. (16 sc)

Rnd 3: (Sc in next st, 2 sc in next st) around. (24 sc)

Rnd 4: (Sc in next 2 sts, 2 sc in next st) around. (32 sc)

Rnd 5: (Sc in next 3 sts, 2 sc in next st) around. (40 sc)

Rnd 6: (Sc in next 4 sts, 2 sc in next st) around. (48 sc)
Rnd 7: (Sc in next 5 sts, 2 sc in next st) around. (56 sc)
Rnd 8: (Sc in next 6 sts, 2 sc in next st) around. (64 sc)
Rnds 9–30: Sc in each st around.
Rnd 31: (Sc in next 6 sts, sc2tog) around. (56 sc)
Rnd 32: Sc in each st around.
Rnd 33: (Sc in next 5 sts, sc2tog) around. (48 sc)
Rnd 34: Sc in each st around.
Rnd 35: (Sc in next 4 sts, sc2tog) around. (40 sc)
Rnd 36: (Sc in next 3 sts, sc2tog) around. (32 sc)
Rnd 37: (Sc in next 2 sts, sc2tog) around. (24 sc)
Stuff Body.

Head

Rnd 38: 2 sc in each st around. (48 sc)
Rnd 39: (Sc in next 5 sts, 2 sc in next st) around. (56 sc)
Rnd 40: (Sc in next 6 sts, 2 sc in next st) around. (64 sc)
Rnds 41–53: Sc in each sc around.
Rnd 54: (Sc in next 6 sts, sc2tog) around. (56 sc)
Add safety eyes between Rnds 50 and 51 about 5 sts apart.
Rnd 55: Sc in each st around.
Rnd 56: (Sc in next 5 sts, sc2tog) around. (48 sc)
Rnd 57: (Sc in next 4 sts, sc2tog) around. (40 sc)
Rnd 58: (Sc in next 3 sts, sc2tog) around. (32 sc)
Rnd 59: (Sc in next 2 sts, sc2tog) around. (24 sc)
Stuff Head.
Rnd 60: (Sc in next st, sc2tog) around. (16 sc)
Rnd 61: (Sc2tog) 8 times. Fasten off, leaving a long tail.
Use yarn needle and long tail to sew Rnd 61 closed.

Wing (make 2)

Note: To work the crocodile stitch: 4 dc down on the next dc post, ch 1, 4 dc up the next post. When all 8 stitches have been completed, it forms a "scale," or "feather," and is considered one "crocodile stitch."
Row 1 (WS): With A, ch 4 (counts as first dc and foundation chain), dc in fourth ch from hook. (2 dc)
Note: This will create a V.
Row 2 (RS): Ch 3 (counts as first dc here and throughout), 3 dc on the last dc post, ch 1, 4 dc up the first (ch 3) post. (8 dc and 1 ch-1 sp = 1 crocodile stitch)
Note 1: You may have to turn your work sideways to work your stitches up and down the posts to create the crocodile stitch.
Note 2: The first crocodile stitch is complete.
Row 3: Ch 3, turn; dc in same st as ch-3 (**Note:** It is on the edge of the crocodile stitch.), 2 dc in the center of crocodile stitch, 2 dc in end/edge of last crocodile stitch. (6 dc)
Row 4: Ch 3, turn, 3 dc on the first dc post, ch 1, 4 dc up the next post, sk 2 sts, crocodile stitch on next 2 dc sts. (2 crocodile stitches)
Row 5: Ch 3, turn, dc in same stitch, 2 dc in the center of the crocodile stitch, 2 dc in unworked 2 dc set (**Note:** When working in this one, work over center of the 2 crocodile stitches from previous row. This pulls it tight and binds the rows together.), 2 dc in center of crocodile stitch, 2 dc in end of crocodile stitch. (10 sts)
Row 6: Ch 3, turn, 3 dc on the first post, ch 1, 4 dc up the next post, *sk 2 sts, crocodile stitch on next 2 dc sts, repeat from * to complete row. (3 crocodile stitches)
Row 7: Ch 3, turn, dc in same stitch, 2 dc in the center of the crocodile stitch, *2 dc in unworked 2 dc set, 2 dc in center of the crocodile stitch, repeat from * to last crocodile stitch, 2 dc in end of crocodile stitch to finish. (14 sts)
Row 8: Ch 3, turn, 3 dc on the first post, ch 1, 4 dc up the next post, *sk 2 sts, crocodile stitch on next 2 dc sts, repeat from * to complete row. (4 crocodile stitches)
Row 9: Ch 1, turn, sl st in center of last crocodile stitch, 2 dc in the center of the crocodile stitch, *2 dc in unworked 2 dc set, 2 dc in center of the crocodile stitch, repeat from * to last crocodile stitch. (10 sts)
Row 10: Rep Row 6.
Row 11: Rep Row 7.
Row 12: Rep Row 8.
Row 13: Ch 1, turn; work sc evenly across Row 12. Fasten off, leaving a long tail for sewing.

Beak

Rnd 1 (RS): With D, ch 2, work 6 sc in second ch from hook, join with slip st to first sc. (6 sc)
Note: Loop a short piece of yarn around any stitch to mark Rnd 1 as right side.
Rnd 2: Ch 1, 2 sc in same st as joining, sc in next st, (2 sc in next st, sc in next st) around, join with slip st to first sc. (9 sc)

Rnd 3: Ch 1, 2 sc in same st as joining, sc in next 2 sts, (2 sc in next st, 2 sc in next st) around, join with slip st to first sc. (12 sc)

Rnd 4: Ch 1, 2 sc in same st as joining, sc in next 5 sts, 2 sc in next st, sc in next 6 sts, join with slip st to first sc. (14 sc)

Rnd 5: Ch 1, 2 sc in same st as joining, sc in next 6 sts, 2 sc in next st, sc in next 7 sts, join with slip st to first sc. (16 sc)

Rnd 6: Ch 1, sc in same st as joining and in each st around, join with slip st to first sc. Fasten off, leaving a long tail for sewing.

Foot (make 2)

Toe (make 6; 3 for each Foot)

Rnd 1 (RS): With B, ch 2, work 4 sc in second ch from hook, do not join. (4 sc) Place marker to indicate beginning of rnd.

Note: Loop a short piece of yarn around any stitch to mark Rnd 1 as right side.

Rnd 2: (Sc, 2 sc in next st) around. (6 sc)

Rnds 3–5: Sc in each st around. Fasten off.

Stuff each Toe.

Foot

Rnd 1 (RS): Working with 3 Toes, join B with slip st in any st of Toe 1, ch 1, sc in same st as joining and in next 2 sts, sc in 3 sts across Toe 2, sc in next 6 sts around Toe 3, sc in next 3 sts across Toe 2, sc in last 3 sts on Toe 1, join with slip st to first sc. (18 sc)

Note: Loop a short piece of yarn around any stitch to mark Rnd 1 as right side.

Rnd 2: Ch 1, sc in same st as joining, sc2tog, (sc in next st, sc2tog) around, join with slip st to first sc. (12 sc)

Rnd 3: Ch 1, sc in same st as joining and in each st around, join with slip st to first sc.

Rnd 4: (Sc2tog) 6 times, join with slip st to first sc. (6 sc)

Rnd 5: Ch 1, sc in same st, join with slip st to first sc.

Stuff Foot.

Fasten off, leaving a long tail for sewing.

Thread yarn needle with long tail and close Rnd 5.

Leg (make 2)

Rnd 1 (RS): With B, ch 6, join with slip st to first ch to create a ring.

Note: Loop a short piece of yarn around any stitch to mark Rnd 1 as right side.

Rnd 2: Ch 1, 6 sc in ring, join with slip st to first sc. (6 sc)

Rnd 3: Ch 1, sc in same st as joining and in each st around, join with slip st to first sc. Fasten off, leaving a long tail for sewing.

Sew Leg on bottom back of Foot.

Stuff Leg.

Comb

Row 1 (RS): With C, ch 31, sc in second ch from hook and in each ch across. (30 sc)

Row 2: Ch 4, turn, (sl st, sc, hdc) in first st, *sk 1 st, (sl st, sc, hdc) in next st; repeat from * across. [7 (sl st, sc, hdc) groups] Fasten off, leaving a long tail for sewing.

Fold in half and sew Row 1 together.

Ruffle Collar

Top

Row 1 (RS): With A, ch 32, sk 3 chs, *ch 3, sk 2 chs, sc in next ch; repeat from * across. Fasten off, leaving a long tail for sewing.

Bottom

Row 1 (RS): With D, ch 32, sc in second ch from hook and in each ch across. (31 sc)

Row 2: Ch 3, sk 2 sts, sc in next sc, *ch 3, sk 2 sts, sc in next st; repeat from * across. Fasten off, leaving a long tail for sewing.

Flower

Top

Rnd 1 (RS): With E, ch 2, work 6 sc in second ch from hook, join with slip st to first sc. (6 sc)

Note: Loop a short piece of yarn around any stitch to mark Rnd 1 as right side.

Rnd 2: (Ch 1, dc, ch 1, sl st) in same st as joining, (sl st, ch 1, dc, ch 1, sl st) in each st around, join with slip st to first sc. (6 petals) Fasten off, leaving a long tail for sewing.

Bottom

Rnd 1 (RS): With E, ch 2, work 7 sc in second ch from hook, join with slip st to first sc. (7 sc)

Rnd 2: (Ch 1, dc, ch 1, sl st) in same st as joining, (sl st, ch 1, dc, ch 1, sl st) in each st around, join with slip st to first sc. (7 petals) Fasten off, leaving a long tail for sewing.

Thread yarn needle with Top long tail and sew to Bottom Flower.

Assembly

Use photos as a guide.

Sew Beak on Head, stuffing before closing.

Thread yarn needle with B, pinch the top of Beak, and stitch in place.

With F, add eyelashes on edges of eyes.

Sew last row of each Wing on Body.

Sew Comb on top of Head.

Sew Bottom Neck Collar around Neck.

Sew Top Collar above Bottom Collar around Neck.

Sew Flower on Body.

Sew Legs on Body.

MASTER THE GOAT

Master the Goat is laser focused. He is super serious, and all of the farm animals line up when they hear him call. His cool hair and goat-tee (okay, it's a beard but I couldn't resist) make him look super cool!

Yarn

Cascade Pacific Chunky; bulky weight #5; 60% acrylic/40% superwash Merino wool; 3.5 oz. (100 g)/120 yd. (110 m) per skein: 3 skeins in 15 Taupe (A); 1 skein each in 10 Cream (B), 153 Ganache (C)

Cascade Cherub Chunky; bulky weight #5; 55% nylon/45% acrylic; 3.5 oz. (100 g)/136.7 yd. (125 m) per skein: 2 skeins in 04 Baby Pink (D), 40 Black (F) (scrap for eyebrows and nose)

Cascade Magnum; super bulky weight #6; 100% Peruvian Highland wool; 8.82 oz. (250 g)/123 yd. (112.5 m) per skein: 1 skein in 10 Ecru (E)

Hook and Other Materials

US size J-10 (6 mm) crochet hook
Yarn needle
Fiberfill stuffing
Two 15 mm safety eyes
Stitch markers

Finished Measurements

About 14½ in. (36.8 cm) high (not counting hair)

Gauge

13 sc and 13 rows/rounds = 4 in. (10 cm)

INSTRUCTIONS

Body

Rnd 1 (RS): With A, ch 2, 8 sc in 2nd ch from hook, do not join. (8 sc) Place marker to indicate beginning of rnd.

Note: Loop a short piece of yarn around any stitch to mark Rnd 1 as right side. Move stitch marker up with each rnd.

Rnd 2: 2 sc in each st around. (16 sc)
Rnd 3: (Sc in next st, 2 sc in next st) around. (24 sc)
Rnd 4: (Sc in next 2 sts, 2 sc in next st) around. (32 sc)
Rnd 5: (Sc in next 3 sts, 2 sc in next st) around. (40 sc)
Rnd 6: (Sc in next 4 sts, 2 sc in next st) around. (48 sc)
Rnd 7: (Sc in next 5 sts, 2 sc in next st) around. (56 sc)
Rnd 8: (Sc in next 6 sts, 2 sc in next st) around. (64 sc)
Rnds 9–30: Sc in each st around.
Rnd 31: (Sc in next 6 sts, sc2tog) around. (56 sc)
Rnd 32: Sc in each st around.
Rnd 33: (Sc in next 5 sts, sc2tog) around. (48 sc)
Rnd 34: Sc in each st around.
Rnd 35: (Sc in next 4 sts, sc2tog) around. (40 sc)
Rnd 36: (Sc in next 3 sts, sc2tog) around. (32 sc)
Rnd 37: (Sc in next 2 sts, sc2tog) around. (24 sc)
Stuff Body.

Head

Rnd 38: 2 sc in each st around. (48 sc)
Rnd 39: (Sc in next 5 sts, 2 sc in next st) around. (56 sc)
Rnd 40: (Sc in next 6 sts, 2 sc in next st) around. (64 sc)
Rnds 41–53: Sc in each sc around.
Rnd 54: (Sc in next 6 sts, sc2tog) around. (56 sc)
Add safety eyes between Rnds 52 and 53 about 5 sts apart.
Rnd 55: Sc in each st around.
Rnd 56: (Sc in next 5 sts, sc2tog) around. (48 sc)
Rnd 57: (Sc in next 4 sts, sc2tog) around. (40 sc)
Rnd 58: (Sc in next 3 sts, sc2tog) around. (32 sc)
Rnd 59: (Sc in next 2 sts, sc2tog) around. (24 sc)
Stuff Head.
Rnd 60: (Sc in next st, sc2tog) around. (16 sc)
Rnd 61: (Sc2tog) 8 times. Fasten off, leaving a long tail.
Use yarn needle and long tail to sew Rnd 61 closed.

Leg (make 2)

Rnd 1 (RS): With B, ch 2, 5 sc in second ch from hook, do not join. (5 sc) Place marker to indicate beginning of rnd.
Note: Loop a short piece of yarn around any stitch to mark Rnd 1 as right side. Move stitch marker up with each rnd.
Rnd 2: 2 sc in each st around. (10 sc)
Rnd 3: (Sc in next st, 2 sc in next st) around. (15 sc)
Rnd 4: (Sc in next 2 sts, 2 sc in next st) around. (20 sc)
Rnd 5: (Sc in next 3 sts, 2 sc in next st) around. (25 sc)
Rnd 6: Sc in each st around. Fasten off.
Rnd 7: Join A with slip st in any st, ch 1, sc2tog, sc in each st around. (24 sc)
Rnd 8: (Sc in next 2 sts, sc2tog) around. (18 sc)
Rnds 9–14: Sc in each st around.
Rnd 15: (Sc in next 7 sts, sc2tog) around. (16 sc)
Rnds 16–23: Sc in each st around. Fasten off, leaving a long tail for sewing.
Stuff firmly at hoof section, lightly stuff Leg, and leave remaining 2½ in. (6.4 cm) unstuffed.

Arm (make 2)

Rnd 1: With B, ch 2, 5 sc in second ch from hook, do not join. (5 sc) Place marker to indicate beginning of rnd.
Note: Loop a short piece of yarn around any stitch to mark Rnd 1 as right side. Move stitch marker up with each rnd.
Rnd 2: 2 sc in each st around. (10 sc)
Rnd 3: (Sc in next st, 2 sc in next st) around. (15 sc)
Rnd 4: (Sc in next 2 sts, 2 sc in next st) around. (20 sc)
Rnd 5: Sc in each st around. Fasten off.
Rnd 6: Join A with slip st in any st, ch 1, sc in same st as joining, sc in next st, sc2tog, (sc in next 2 sts, sc2tog) around. (15 sc)
Rnds 7–22: Sc in each st around. Fasten off, leaving a long tail for sewing.
Stuff firmly at hoof section, lightly stuff Arm, and leave remaining 2½ in. (6.4 cm) unstuffed.

Horn (make 2)

Rnd 1 (RS): With C, ch 2, 4 sc in second ch from hook, do not join. (4 sc) Place marker to indicate beginning of rnd.
Note: Loop a short piece of yarn around any stitch to mark Rnd 1 as right side. Move stitch marker up with each rnd.
Rnd 2: 2 sc in each st around. (8 sc)
Rnds 3 and 4: Sc in each st around. Fasten off, leaving a long tail for sewing.
Stuff Horn.

Ear (make 2)

Rnd 1: With A, ch 2, work 4 sc in second ch from hook, do not join. (4 sc) Place marker to indicate beginning of rnd.

Note: Loop a short piece of yarn around any stitch to mark Rnd 1 as right side. Move stitch marker up with each rnd.
Rnd 2: 2 sc in each st around. (8 sc)
Rnd 3: Sc in each st around.
Rnd 4: (Sc in next st, 2 sc in next st) around. (12 sc)
Rnd 5: Sc in each st around.
Rnd 6: (Sc in next 2 sts, 2 sc in next st) around. (16 sc)
Rnd 7: Sc in each st around.
Rnd 8: (Sc in next 3 sts, 2 sc in next st) around. (20 sc)
Rnds 9–12: Sc in each st around.
Rnd 13: (Sc in next 3 sts, sc2tog) around. (16 sc)
Rnd 14: (Sc in next 2 sts, sc2tog) around. (12 sc) Fasten off, leaving a long tail for sewing.
Do not stuff.

Inner Ear (make 2)

Row 1 (RS): With D, ch 2, 2 sc in second ch from hook. (2 sc)
Note: Loop a short piece of yarn around any stitch to mark Row 1 as right side.
Row 2: Ch 1, turn; 2 sc in first st, sc in next st. (3 sc)
Rows 3–5: Ch 1, turn; sc in each st across.
Row 6: Ch 1, turn; beginning with first st, sc2tog, sc in next st. (2 sc)
Trim: Ch 1, turn; sc in next 2 sts, work 6 sc in ends of rows, sc in next 2 sts across foundation ch of Row, work 6 sc in ends of rows, join with slip st to first sc. (16 sc) Fasten off, leaving a long tail for sewing.

Snout

Rnd 1 (RS): With B, ch 2, work 6 sc in second ch from hook, join with slip st to first sc (6 sc) Place marker to indicate beginning of rnd.
Note: Loop a short piece of yarn around any stitch to mark Rnd 1 as right side.
Rnd 2: Ch 1, 2 sc in same st as joining, 2 sc in each st around, join with slip st to first sc. (12 sc)
Rnd 3: Ch 1, sc in same st as joining, 2 sc in next st, (sc in next st, 2 sc in next st) around, join with slip st to first st. (18 sc)
Rnds 4 and 5: Ch 1, sc in same st as joining and in each st around, join with slip st to first sc. Fasten off.
Rnd 6: Join A with slip st, ch 1, sc in same st as joining and in next st, 2 sc in next st, (sc in next 2 sts, 2 sc in next st) around, join with slip st to first sc. (24 sc)
Rnd 7: Ch 1, sc in same st as joining and in next 2 sts, 2 sc in next st, (sc in next 3 sts, 2 sc in next st) around, join with slip st to first sc. (30 sc) Fasten off, leaving a long tail for sewing.
Thread yarn needle with F and stitch on nose and mouth.

Assembly

Use photos as a guide.
Sew Snout on Head, stuffing before closing.
With F, add eyebrows above eyes.
Sew Inner Ear to Ear.
Sew Ears on Head.
Sew Horns on Head.
Sew Arms and Legs on Body.
Tack Legs to Body to hold in place.

Beard

Cut six strands of E, each 8 in. (20.3 cm) long. Split yarn 3 times.
Add as fringe under Snout on Rnds 6 and 7. To do this, fold yarn in half. Pull loop through stitches under the Snout. Pull ends through loop and tighten.
Comb lightly and trim.

Hair

Cut 10 strands of E, each 8 in. (20.3 cm) long. Split yarn 3 times.
Add as fringe as for Beard, in a triangle pattern starting 6 rounds above eyes.
Comb lightly and trim.

Tail

Cut 4 strands of E, each 8 in. (20.3 cm) long. Split yarn 3 times.
Add as fringe to lower back of Body. Brush upwards and trim.

QUACKERS THE DUCK

Quackers is a crowd favorite. He has his own duck call, so you can find him anytime! He's never too far from the chicken coop and loves feeding time with his friends. Pick him up for a quick snuggle!

Yarn

Cascade Pacific Chunky; bulky weight #5; 60% acrylic/40% superwash Merino wool; 3.5 oz. (100 g)/120 yd. (110 m) per skein: 1 skein each in 166 Toasted Coconut (A), 153 Ganache (B), 185 Duck Green (C), 167 Marmalade (D), 13 Gold (E)

Cascade Anthem Chunky; bulky weight #5; 100% acrylic; 7.05 oz. (200 g)/218 yd. (200 m) per skein: 1 skein: 41 Denim (F)

Hook and Other Materials

US size J-10 (6 mm) crochet hook
Yarn needle
Fiberfill stuffing
Two 15 mm safety eyes
Stitch markers

Finished Measurements

About 13 in. (33 cm) high (not counting hair)

Gauge

13 sc and 13 rows/rounds = 4 in. (10 cm)

INSTRUCTIONS

Body

Rnd 1 (RS): With A, ch 2, 8 sc in 2nd ch from hook, do not join. (8 sc) Place marker to indicate beginning of rnd.

Note: Loop a short piece of yarn around any stitch to mark Rnd 1 as right side. Move stitch marker up with each rnd.

Rnd 2: 2 sc in each st around. (16 sc)

Rnd 3: (Sc in next st, 2 sc in next st) around. (24 sc)

Rnd 4: (Sc in next 2 sts, 2 sc in next st) around. (32 sc)

Rnd 5: (Sc in next 3 sts, 2 sc in next st) around. (40 sc)
Rnd 6: (Sc in next 4 sts, 2 sc in next st) around. (48 sc)
Rnd 7: (Sc in next 5 sts, 2 sc in next st) around. (56 sc)
Rnd 8: (Sc in next 6 sts, 2 sc in next st) around. (64 sc)
Rnds 9–23: Sc in each st around.
Rnd 24: (Sc in next 6 sts, sc2tog) around. (56 sc)
Rnd 25: Sc in each st around.
Rnd 26: Sc in each st around; join with slip st to first sc. Fasten off.
Rnd 27: Join B with slip st, ch 1, sc in same st as joining and in next 4 sts, sc2tog, (sc in next 5 sts, sc2tog) around. (48 sc)
Rnd 28: Sc in each st around.
Rnd 29: (Sc in next 4 sts, sc2tog) around. (40 sc)
Rnd 30: Sc in each st around.
Rnd 31: (Sc in next 3 sts, sc2tog) around. (32 sc)
Rnd 32: Sc in each st around.
Rnd 33: (Sc in next 2 sts, sc2tog) around. (24 sc) Fasten off.
Stuff Body.

Head

Rnd 34: Join C with slip st, ch 1, 2 sc in same st as joining, 2 sc in each st around. (48 sc)
Rnd 35: (Sc in next 5 sts, 2 sc in next st) around. (56 sc)
Rnd 36: (Sc in next 6 sts, 2 sc in next st) around. (64 sc)
Rnd 37: (Sc in next 7 sts, 2 sc in next st) around. (72 sc)
Rnds 38–40: Sc in each st around.
Rnd 41: (Sc in next 7 sts, sc2tog) around. (64 sc)
Rnd 42: Sc in each st around.
Rnd 43: (Sc in next 6 sts, sc2tog) around. (56 sc)
Rnd 44: Sc in each st around.
Rnd 45: (Sc in next 5 sts, sc2tog) around. (48 sc)
Rnd 46: Sc in each st around.
Rnd 47: (Sc in next 4 sts, sc2tog) around. (40 sc)
Rnds 48–50: Sc in each st around.
Rnd 51: (Sc in next 3 sts, sc2tog) around. (32 sc)
Add safety eyes between Rnds 45 and 46 about 5 sts apart.
Rnd 52: Sc in each st around.
Rnd 53: (Sc in next 2 sts, sc2tog) around. (24 sc)
Rnd 54: Sc in each st around.
Stuff Head.
Rnd 55: (Sc in next st, sc2tog) around. (16 sc)
Rnd 56: Sc in each st around.

Rnd 57: (Sc2tog) 8 times. (8 sc) Fasten off, leaving a long tail.
Use yarn needle and long tail to sew Rnd 57 closed.

Wing 1

Rnd 1 (RS): With B, ch 2, 6 sc in second ch from hook, do not join. (6 sc) Place marker to indicate beginning of rnd.
Note: Loop a short piece of yarn around any stitch to mark Rnd 1 as right side. Move stitch marker up with each rnd.
Rnd 2: 2 sc in each st around. (12 sc)
Rnd 3: (Sc in next st, 2 sc in next st) around. (18 sc)
Rnd 4: (Sc in next 2 sts, 2 sc in next st) around. (24 sc)
Rnd 5: (Sc in next 3 sts, 2 sc in next st) around. (30 sc)
Rnd 6: (Sc in next 4 sts, 2 sc in next st) around. (36 sc)
Rnd 7: (Sc in next 5 sts, 2 sc in next st) around. (42 sc)
Rnd 8: (Sc in next 6 sts, 2 sc in next st) around. (48 sc)

Rnd 9: (Sc in next 7 sts, 2 sc in next st) 3 times, (sk 1 st, 4 dc in next st, sk 1 st, sl st in next st) 6 times, join with slip st to first sc. Fasten off, leaving a long tail for sewing.

Fold in half and sew the smooth edge of Rnd 9 to back and bottom of scallops.

Wing 2

Repeat Rnds 1–8 of Wing 1.

Rnd 9: (Sk 1 st, 4 dc in next st, sk 1 st, sl st in next st) 6 times, (sc in next 7 sts, 2 sc in next st) 3 times, join with slip st to first sc. Fasten off, leaving a long tail for sewing.

Fold in half and sew the smooth edge of Rnd 9 to back and bottom of scallops.

Bill

Rnd 1 (RS): With E, ch 8, 2 sc in second ch from hook, sc in next 5 chs, 4 sc in last ch, working on opposite side of ch in free loops, sc in next 5 chs, 2 sc in last ch, join with slip st to first sc. (18 sc)

Note: Loop a short piece of yarn around any stitch to mark Rnd 1 as right side.

Rnds 2 and 3: Ch 1, sc in same st as joining and in each st around, join with slip st to first sc.

Rnd 4: Ch 1, 2 sc in same st as joining, sc in next 7 sts, 2 sc in next 2 sts, sc in next 7 sts, 2 sc in last st, join with slip st to first sc. (22 sc)

Rnds 5 and 6: Ch 1, sc in same st as joining and in each st around, join with slip st to first sc. Fasten off, leaving a long tail for sewing.

Stuff Bill.

Foot (make 4)

Row 1 (RS): With D, ch 5, sc in second ch from hook and in each ch across. (4 sc)

Note: Loop a short piece of yarn around any stitch to mark Row 1 as right side.

Row 2: Ch 1, turn; 2 sc in first st, sc in next 2 sts, 2 sc in last st. (6 sc)

Row 3: Ch 1, turn; sc in each st across.

Row 4: Ch 1, turn; 2 sc in first st, sc in next 4 sts, 2 sc in last st. (8 sc)

Row 5: Ch 1, turn; sc in each st across.

Row 6: Ch 1, turn; 2 sc in first st, sc in next 6 sts, 2 sc in last st. (10 sc)

Rows 7 and 8: Ch 1, turn; sc in each st across.

Row 9: Ch 1, turn; (dc, ch 1) in same st, sc in next st, hdc in next st, sk 1 st, (3 dc, ch 1) in next st, 3 dc in next st, sk 1 st, hdc in next st, sc in next st, (ch 1, dc) in last st. Fasten off, leaving a long tail for sewing.

Placing wrong sides together, sew 2 Feet together around the edge. Repeat for second Foot.

Leg (make 2)

Rnd 1 (RS): With D, ch 6, join with slip st to first ch to create a ring.

Note: Loop a short piece of yarn around any stitch to mark Rnd 1 as right side.

Rnd 2: Ch 1, 8 sc in ring, join with slip st to first sc. (8 sc)

Rnd 3: Ch 1, sc in same st as joining and in each st around, join with slip st to first sc. Fasten off, leave a long tail for sewing.

Duck Call

Part 1

Row 1 (RS): With E, ch 4, sc in second ch from hook and in next 2 chs. (3 sc)

Note: Loop a short piece of yarn around any stitch to mark Row 1 as right side.

Rows 2 and 3: Ch 1, sc in each st across. Fasten off, leaving a long tail for sewing.

Thread yarn needle with long tail and sew Row 1 to Row 3.

Part 2

Rnd 1 (RS): Join F with slip st in the end of any row, work 4 slip st around, join with slip st to first st. (4)

Note: Loop a short piece of yarn around any stitch to mark Rnd 1 as right side.

Rnd 2: Ch 1, working in blo, sc in same st as joining and in each st around, join with slip st to first sc.

Rnd 3: Ch 1, sc in same st as joining and in each st around, join with slip st to first sc. Fasten off.

Assembly

Use photos as a guide.

Sew Bill on Head, stuffing before closing.

Sew Wings on Body with scallop edging on the inside.

Sew each Foot to a Leg.

Sew Legs on Body, tacking middle point of Foot to Body.

Hair

Cut eight strands of C, each 6 in. (15.2 cm) long.

Add as fringe at top of Head by folding each strand in half and pulling loop through a stitch. Pull ends through the middle loop and tighten. Repeat. Trim.

MELA THE HIGHLAND COW

This Highland cow is the coolest cow on the farm. Her buddies are always close by and love roaming around grazing together. They have the neatest shaggy hair (that is made by creating loop stitches and cutting . . . no extra fringe!) that makes them look so chill and fun! Mela is super curious and wants to have all the treats and pets.

Yarn

Cascade Pacific Chunky; bulky weight #5; 60% acrylic/40% superwash Merino wool; 3.5 oz. (100 g)/120 yd. (110 m) per skein: 3 skeins in 158 Copper Brown (A); 1 skein each in 1 Cream (B), 153 Ganache (C)

Hook and Other Materials

US size J-10 (6 mm) crochet hook
Yarn needle
Fiberfill stuffing
Two 15 mm safety eyes
Stitch markers

Finished Measurements

About 15 in. (38 cm) high (not counting horns)

Gauge

13 sc and 13 rows/rounds = 4 in. (10 cm)

Special Stitch

Loop Stitch (Loop st): YO, wrap working yarn around thumb and pull down, place the hook *over* the yarn and into the stitch, YO and pull up a loop (3 loops on hook), YO and pull through all 3 loops.

Note: When cut, it will look like fringe and not be loose.

How to Work Loop Stitch

1. Yarn over.

2. Wrap the working yarn around your thumb as shown and pull down.

3. Place the hook *over* the yarn and into the stitch.

4. Yarn over and pull up a loop. Three loops on hook.

5. Yarn over and pull through all 3 loops.

INSTRUCTIONS

Body

Rnd 1 (RS): With A, ch 2, 8 sc in second ch from hook, do not join. (8 sc) Place marker to indicate beginning of rnd.

Note: Loop a short piece of yarn around any stitch to mark Rnd 1 as right side. Move stitch marker up with each rnd.

Rnd 2: 2 sc in each st around. (16 sc)

Rnd 3: (Sc in next st, 2 sc in next st) around. (24 sc)

Rnd 4: (Sc in next 2 sts, 2 sc in next st) around. (32 sc)

Rnd 5: (Sc in next 3 sts, 2 sc in next st) around. (40 sc)

Rnd 6: (Sc in next 4 sts, 2 sc in next st) around. (48 sc)

Rnd 7: (Sc in next 5 sts, 2 sc in next st) around. (56 sc)

Rnd 8: (Sc in next 6 sts, 2 sc in next st) around. (64 sc)

Rnd 9: Sc in each st around.

Rnd 10: (Sc in next 7 sts, 2 sc in next st) around. (72 sc)

Rnds 11–15: Sc in each st around.

Rnd 16: Loop st in each st around.

Rnds 17–19: Sc in each st around.

Rnd 20: Loop st in each st around.

Rnds 21–23: Sc in each st around.

Rnd 24: Loop st in each st around.

Rnd 25: (Sc in next 7 sts, sc2tog) around. (64 sc)

Rnd 26: Sc in each st around.

Rnd 27: Loop st in each st around.

Rnd 28: (Sc in next 6 sts, sc2tog) around. (56 sc)

Rnds 29 and 30: Sc in each st around.

Rnd 31: Loop st in each st around.

Rnd 32: (Sc in next 5 sts, sc2tog) around. (48 sc)

Rnd 33: Sc in each st around.

Rnd 34: Loop st in each st around.

Rnd 35: (Sc in next 4 sts, sc2tog) around. (40 sc)

Rnd 36: Sc in each st around.

Rnd 37: Loop st in each st around.

Rnd 38: (Sc in next 3 sts, sc2tog) around. (32 sc)

Rnd 39: (Sc in next 2 sts, sc2tog) around. (24 sc)

Rnd 40: Loop st in each st around. Fasten off.

Stuff Body firmly.

Cut each Loop St to create fur.

Head

Rnd 1 (RS): With A, ch 2, 6 sc in ring, do not join. (6 sc) Place marker to indicate beginning of rnd.

Note: Loop a short piece of yarn around any stitch to mark Rnd 1 as right side. Move stitch marker up with each rnd.

Rnd 2: Work 2 Loop sts in each st around. (12 sc)

Rnd 3: (Sc in next st, 2 sc in next st) around. (18 sc)

Rnd 4: (Sc in next 2 sts, 2 sc in next st) around. (24 sc)

Rnd 5: (Loop st in next 3 sts, 2 Loop sts in next st) around. (30 sts)

Rnd 6: (Sc in next 4 sts, 2 sc in next st) around. (36 sc)

Rnd 7: Sc in each st around.

Rnd 8: (Loop st in next 5 sts, 2 Loop sts in next st) around. (42 sc)

Rnd 9: (Sc in next 6 sts, 2 sc in next st) around. (48 sc)

Rnd 10: (Sc in next 7 sts, 2 sc in next st) around. (54 sc)

Rnd 11: (Loop st in next 8 sts, 2 Loop sts in next st) around. (60 sc)

Rnds 12 and 13: Sc in each st around.

Rnd 14: Loop st in each st around.

Rnds 15 and 16: Sc in each st around.

Rnd 17: Loop st in each st around.

Rnd 18 and 19: Sc in each st around.

Rnd 20: Loop st in each st around.

Rnd 21: Working in blo, (sc in next 8 sts, sc2tog) around. (54 sc)

Rnd 22: (Sc in next 7 sts, sc2tog) around. (48 sc)

Rnd 23: Sc in each st around.

Rnd 24: (Sc in next 6 sts, sc2tog) around. (42 sc)

Rnd 25: (Sc in next 5 sts, sc2tog) around. (36 sc)

Rnd 26: Sc in each st around.

Rnd 27: (Sc in next 4 sts, sc2tog) around. (30 sc)

Rnd 28: Sc in each st around. Fasten off A.

Stuff Head.

Cut each Loop St.

Nose

Rnd 29: Join B with slip st, ch 1, working in blo, sc in each st around, join with slip st to first st.

Rnds 30 and 31: Ch 1, sc in same st as joining and in each st around, join with slip st to first sc.

Rnd 32: Ch 1, sc in same st as joining and in next st, sc2tog, sc in next 7 sts, sc2tog, sc in next 4 sts, sc2tog, sc in next 7 sts, sc2tog, sc in last 2 sts, join with slip st to first st. (26 sc)

Rnd 33: Ch 1, sc in same st as joining, sc2tog, sc in next 7 sts, sc2tog, sc in next 2 sts, sc2tog, sc in next 7 sts, sc2tog, sc in last st, join with slip st to first sc. (22 sc)

Rnd 34: Ch 1, sc in same st as joining, sc2tog, sc in next 5 sts, sc2tog, sc in next 2 sts, sc2tog, sc in next 5 sts, sc2tog, sc in last st, join with slip st to first sc. (18 sc)

Rnd 35: Ch 1, beginning with same st as joining, sc2tog, sc in next 5 sts, (sc2tog) twice, sc in next 5 sts, sc2tog, join with slip st to first sc. (14 sc)

Stuff Nose.

Add safety eyes between Rnds 26 and 27, about 5 sts apart.

Fasten off, leaving a long tail for sewing.

Thread yarn needle with long tail and sew Rnd 35 closed evenly.

Ear (make 2)

Rnd 1 (RS): With C, ch 4, 9 dc in fourth ch from hook. (10 dc)

Note: Loop a short piece of yarn around any stitch to mark Rnd 1 as right side.

Rnd 2: Ch 1, turn, 2 sc in first st, sc in next st, 2 sc in next st, sc in next st, 2 sc in next 2 sts, (sc in next st, 2 sc in next st) twice. (16 sc)

Rnd 3: Ch 3 (counts as first dc), turn; dc in same st, dc in next st, (2 dc in next st, dc in next st) across. (24 dc). Fasten off, leaving a long tail for sewing.

Thread yarn needle with long tail, fold edge of Rnd 3 together and sew together. Do not fasten off.

Horn (make 2)

Rnd 1 (RS): With B, ch 2, 3 sc in second ch from hook, do not join. (3 sc) Place marker to indicate beginning of rnd.

Note: Loop a short piece of yarn around any stitch to mark Rnd 1 as right side. Move stitch marker up with each rnd.

Rnd 2: Sc in each st around.

Rnd 3: 2 sc in next st, sc in next 2 sts. (4 sc)

Rnd 4: 2 sc in next st, sc in next 3 sts. (5 sc)

Rnd 5: 2 sc in next st, sc in next 4 sts. (6 sc)

Rnd 6: 2 sc in next st, sc in next 5 sts. (7 sc)

Rnd 7: 2 sc in next st, sc in next 6 sts. (8 sc)

Rnd 8: 2 sc in next st, sc in next 7 sts. (9 sc)

Rnd 9: 2 sc in next st, sc in next 8 sts. (10 sc)

Rnd 10: 2 sc in next st, sc in next 9 sts. (11 sc)

Rnd 11: 2 sc in next st, sc in next 10 sts. (12 sc)

Rnd 12: (2 sc in next st, sc in next 3 sts) around. (15 sc)

Rnds 13 and 14: Sc in each st around.

Rnd 15: (Sc2tog, sc in next 3 sts) around, join with slip st to first sc. (12 sc) Fasten off, leaving a long tail for sewing.

Leg (make 2)

Rnd 1 (RS): With C, ch 2, 6 sc in second ch from hook, do not join. (6 sc) Place marker to indicate beginning of rnd.

Note: Loop a short piece of yarn around any stitch to mark Rnd 1 as right side. Move stitch marker up with each rnd.

Rnd 2: 2 sc in each st around. (12 sc)

Rnd 3: (Sc in next st, 2 sc in next st) around. (18 sc)

Rnd 4: (Sc in next 2 sts, 2 sc in next st) around. (24 sc)

Rnds 5–10: Sc in each st around. Fasten off.

Rnd 11: Join B with slip st in any st, ch 1, (sc in next 2 sts, sc2tog) around. (18 sc)

Rnds 12–25: Sc in each st around. Fasten off, leaving a long tail for sewing.

Stuff firmly at hoof section, lightly stuff Leg, and leave remaining 2½ in. (6.4 cm) unstuffed.

Arm (make 2)

Rnd 1: With C, ch 2, 6 sc in second ch from hook, do not join. (6 sc) Place marker to indicate beginning of rnd.

Note: Loop a short piece of yarn around any stitch to mark Rnd 1 as right side. Move stitch marker up with each rnd.

Rnd 2: 2 sc in each st around. (12 sc)

Rnd 3: (Sc in next st, 2 sc in next st) around. (18 sc)

Rnds 4–8: Sc in each st around. Fasten off.

Rnds 9–21: Join A with slip st in any st, ch 1, sc in each st around.

Fasten off, leaving a long tail for sewing.

Stuff firmly at hoof section, lightly stuff Arm, and leave remaining 2½ in. (6.4 cm) unstuffed.

Assembly

Use photos as a guide.

Sew Head to Body.

Sew Horns on Head.

Sew Ear right under the Horn.

Sew Arms and Legs on Body.

Tack Legs to Body to hold in place.

Stitch nostrils on Nose.

Cut each loop stitch.

Use a wide-tooth comb and lightly comb out the ends of the cut yarn.

Nose Detail

Rnd 1: Hold Cow upside down, Join A on bottom of Nose with slip st on exposed loop of Rnd 29, slip st in each exposed loop around, join with slip st to first st. Fasten off.

Tail

Cut 6 strands of A, each 12 in. (30.4 cm) long.

Fold in half, pull loop through stitch in lower back of Body, pull ends through loop and tighten. Separate ends into 3 even sections and braid. Knot and trim.

Bangs

Cut 20 strands of A, each 5 in. (12.5 cm) long.

Add as fringe in same way as for Tail around top and sides on exposed front loops on Head from Rnd 21. Trim as needed. Comb ends lightly.

Fill in any open spots on back of Head as needed with fringe. Trim.

Stitch Guide

SLIPKNOT

This adjustable knot will begin every crochet project.

1. Make a loop in the yarn.

2. With crochet hook or finger, grab the yarn from the skein and pull through the loop.

3. Pull tight on the yarn and adjust to create the first loop.

CHAIN (CH)

The chain provides the foundation for your stitches at the beginning of a pattern. It can also serve as a stitch within a pattern and can be used to create an open effect.

1. Insert the hook through the slipknot and place the yarn over the hook by passing the hook in front of the yarn.

2. Keeping the yarn taut (but not too tight) pull the hook back through the loop with the yarn. Ch 1 is complete.

3. Repeat Steps 1 and 2 to create multiple chains.

SINGLE CROCHET (SC)

1. Insert the hook from the front of the stitch to the back and yarn over.

2. Pull the yarn back through the stitch: 2 loops on the hook.

3. Yarn over and draw through both loops on the hook to complete.

WORKING INTO A STITCH

Unless specified otherwise, you will insert your hook under both loops to crochet any stitch.

WORKING INTO BACK LOOP OR FRONT LOOP

At times you will be instructed to work in the flo or the blo of a stitch to create a texture within the pattern.

Inserting hook to crochet into the flo of a stitch.

Inserting hook to crochet into the blo of a stitch.

SLIP STITCH (SL ST)

The slip stitch is used to join one stitch to another or to join a stitch to another point. It can also be used within the pattern as a stitch without height.

1. Insert the hook from the front of the stitch to the back of the stitch and yarn over.

2. Pull the yarn back through the stitch: 2 loops on the hook.

3. Continue to pull the loop through the first loop on the hook to finish.

HALF DOUBLE CROCHET (HDC)

1. Yarn over from the back to the front over the hook.

2. Insert the hook from the front of the stitch to the back.

3. Yarn over and pull the yarn back through the stitch: 3 loops on the hook.

4. Yarn over and draw through all 3 loops on the hook to complete.

DOUBLE CROCHET (DC)

1. Yarn over and insert the hook from the front of the stitch to the back.

2. Yarn over and pull the yarn back through the stitch: 3 loops on the hook.

3. Yarn over and draw the yarn through the first 2 loops on the hook: 2 loops on the hook.

4. Yarn over and draw the yarn through the last 2 loops on the hook to complete.

INVISIBLE SINGLE CROCHET 2 TOGETHER (SC2TOG)

When working within a pattern, use the invisible single crochet 2 together when sc2tog is used to create a less visible decrease:

1. Insert the hook in the flo of the next 2 stitches and yarn over.

2. Draw through both stitches, yarn over, and draw through 2 loops on the hook (counts as one sc).

INVISIBLE JOIN

1. Complete your last stitch, cut the yarn leaving a long end, and pull the yarn all the way through the last stitch/loop.

2. Thread the needle with the long end, skip 1 stitch, and insert the yarn needle from the front to the back of the next stitch.

3. Skip the skipped stitch and insert the yarn needle into the last stitch in the back loop from left to right (photo shows which back loop to use, but not in the proper direction; insert left to right).

4. Pull the yarn loosely to create a new loop over the skipped loop. Photo shows how the invisible join creates a "loop" to finish the work. Weave in the ends on the wrong side of the work.

MAGIC RING

1. Hold the end of the yarn with pinky and ring fingers, and wrap the yarn around the pointer finger as shown.

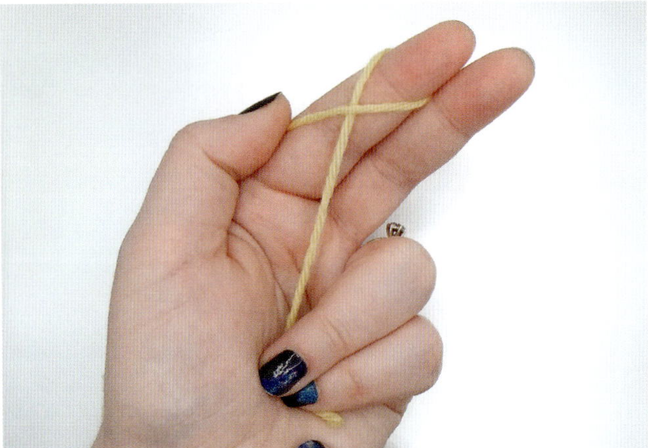

2. Insert the hook through the loop on pointer finger and pull up the loop.

3. Chain one. This is an important step.

4. Follow the pattern and crochet into the loop and *over* the tail at the same time.

5. When you have completed the pattern directions, pull the beginning yarn tail until the center opening is tight and closed. Knot on the wrong side to hold in place securely.

COLOR CHANGE

When changing colors without fastening off, use this technique:

1. Execute your given stitch up to the last pull-through.

2. Yarn over with the next color, and pull through to finish the stitch and color change. Cut or drop the yarn from the original color.

3. Continue working with joined color.

Acknowledgments

A special thank-you to Kim Simpson for being my right hand and taking pride in our craft. I am proud to share this book with you and mentor you in the writing process. Here's to many more collaborations. Your dad and I love you.

Thanks to Ciji Bates and her two kiddos, Luke and Tessa, and Abbie Clemons and her family (a huge shout-out to Eliza and Everly) for braving the farm with me for photos. It was a great day, and I appreciate your willingness to model for this book.

Another thanks to Abbie for being my photo assistant. With so many kiddos and animals running around, the extra set of hands was much appreciated!

And last, but not least, many thanks to my husband. You're the best. I mean, you support me playing with yarn! You helped with this book more than you know—from yarn colors and designs to just me bouncing a million ideas off you—you're awesome! I love you more.